M000087205

UNBREAKABLE

UNBREAKABLE

READINGS
that
INSPIRE
and
MOTIVATE

Dr. Carolyn Vincent

authorHOUSE®

AuthorHouse™
1663 Liberty Drive
Bloomington, IN 47403
www.authorhouse.com
Phone: 833-262-8899

© 2021 Dr. Carolyn Vincent. All rights reserved.
Cover and interior design: Adina Cucicov

No part of this book may be reproduced, stored in a retrieval system, or
transmitted by any means without the written permission of the author.

Published by AuthorHouse 04/29/2021

ISBN: 978-1-6655-1692-1 (sc)
ISBN: 978-1-6655-1690-7 (hc)
ISBN: 978-1-6655-1691-4 (e)

Library of Congress Control Number: 2021902894

Print information available on the last page.

Any people depicted in stock imagery provided by Getty Images are models,
and such images are being used for illustrative purposes only.
Certain stock imagery © Getty Images.

Cover Photo by © Pei Ling Hoo (www.123rf.com)

This book is printed on acid-free paper.

Because of the dynamic nature of the Internet, any web addresses or
links contained in this book may have changed since publication and
may no longer be valid. The views expressed in this work are solely those
of the author and do not necessarily reflect the views of the publisher,
and the publisher hereby disclaims any responsibility for them.

*I dedicate this book to the person who
has had the most significant impact on my life—
my mother, Johnnie Mae Vincent aka Madea.
She departed this earthly life on October 10, 2020.
Without her love, prayers, encouragement, and
guidance, I would not be the person I am today.
I'm honored to be her daughter.*

CONTENTS

Acknowledgements ◆ ◆ ◆ *ix*

Introduction ◆ ◆ ◆ *1*

Spring is in the air ◆ ◆ ◆ *2*

This moment ◆ ◆ ◆ *4*

It's not the truth ◆ ◆ ◆ *6*

I will be ready ◆ ◆ ◆ *8*

Sister-friend ◆ ◆ ◆ *12*

This time is different ◆ ◆ ◆ *14*

The power of love ◆ ◆ ◆ *16*

Thrill of excitement ◆ ◆ ◆ *18*

Do you see me? ◆ ◆ ◆ *20*

Already yours ◆ ◆ ◆ *24*

Kindness makes a difference ◆ ◆ ◆ *26*

Love unconditionally ◆ ◆ ◆ *28*

By your actions ◆ ◆ ◆ *30*

The man that you are ◆ ◆ ◆ *32*

Think big ◆ ◆ ◆ *34*

Using what I have ◆ ◆ ◆ *36*

Where is your backyard? ◆ ◆ ◆ *38*

Worth the effort ◆ ◆ ◆ *40*

You helped me today ◆ ◆ ◆ *42*

Chart new territory ◆ ◆ ◆ *44*

Amazing success ••• 46

Showing up ••• 48

Grow through your wilderness ••• 50

My destiny ••• 52

Even stronger ••• 56

Great expectation ••• 58

If you knew ••• 60

It's time ••• 62

Enjoying each moment ••• 64

One that loves me most ••• 66

Thorn in my side ••• 68

Preparation time ••• 70

As I experience ••• 72

When you are excited ••• 74

Not without a price ••• 76

I am still here ••• 78

Standing still ••• 80

You deserve it ••• 82

It takes courage ••• 84

I am positioned ••• 86

Flicker of light ••• 88

I have to love me too ••• 90

Finally ••• 94

Come back stronger ••• 96

God's kindness ••• 98

The gift of you ••• 100

Incredibly you ••• 102

Higher purpose ••• 104

See yourself ••• 106

In the stillness ••• 108

ACKNOWLEDGEMENTS

To all of the people I have encountered along this journey. I have learned so much from each of you. You were the vessels chosen to teach me the lessons I needed to learn and grow. I will be eternally grateful for each moment shared with you.

My mom and dad (both deceased) who were the best role models I could ever have. Thank you for teaching me the meaning of unconditional love. You gave me the tools I needed to be successful. You taught me how to be resilient and how to persevere. Thank you for inspiring me every day.

My brother LeRoy who is also with the heavenly father. You kept a poem that I wrote you over 30 years ago, so it truly fills my heart to know that I have a great champion in you.

My husband Brady for being my greatest champion and supporter. Thank you for being by my side. Your love and support mean the world to me.

I owe my sincere gratitude and thanks to all of my family, friends, and the kind strangers who have encourage me to publish my readings. You helped me to see the impact my readings have on others. Without you, I'm not sure if I would be taking this step.

- To anyone who is looking for hope and encouragement. Like you, I have had my share of disappointments and challenges, but I am still here. You are too so please don't give up now! My prayer is that these readings will provide you with insight and guidance while giving you the motivation you need to move forward.

INTRODUCTION

Unbreakable: *Readings that Inspire and Motivate* speaks to our ability to persevere in spite of the obstacles we face. Its purpose is to encourage, uplift, and offer hope for a better tomorrow. I hope that you will see that no matter where you are in your journey—there is always hope. There is always an opportunity to improve and grow. You may have been shattered, you may have been bruised, you may have even been knocked down but you did not break because you are Unbreakable!

SPRING IS IN THE AIR

Spring is in the air!
I hear it in the birds chirping as if they are singing a song.
I see it in the magnificent blue sky with the promise of better
    days.
I feel it in the rays of the sun shining gloriously with the hope of
    a brighter future.
Spring is in the air!
I hear it in the voices of those I encounter.
I sense it in the positive energy from being around others.
I embrace it with the words of encouragement and support that
        I receive.
Spring is in the air!
And I am looking forward to all the opportunities that it will bring.
I am excited about all the possibilities that it will present.
I am energized by the prospect of doing and being.
Spring is in the air!
So, with great enthusiasm and zeal—I anxiously await its arrival!

Insights & Reflections

THIS MOMENT

My journey has prepared me for this moment.
To excel and soar like the eagle that I am,
To triumph and overcome every obstacle I encounter,
To see the gift in each disappointment,
To embrace the learning in spite of what appears to be a failure,
My journey has prepared me for this moment.
To walk in the path that only I am destined to travel,
To recognize the greatness and power that I embody,
To be fearless and courageous in the face of uncertainty,
To walk boldly with each passing day,
My journey has prepared me for this moment.
To remain vigilant especially when I feel wary,
To seize each opportunity as though it were my last,
To be joyful and thankful in all things,
To recognize the gifts that each of us offer,
My journey has prepared me for this moment.

Insights & Reflections

IT'S NOT THE TRUTH

Just because you have some doubts does not mean your faith
is weak.
Just because you have insecurities does not mean you are not
confident.
Just because you have fears does not mean you cannot
move forward.
It just means that you have work to do because what you feel
right now,
Is not the truth about you.
Just because you feel like you are struggling constantly does not
mean that you will not survive.
Just because you sometimes feel alone does not mean you do not
have support.
Just because you feel surrounded by problems does not mean
you do not have the solution.
It just means you have work to do because what you feel right now,
Is not the truth about you.
Just because you are hard on yourself does not mean you deserve
such treatment.
Just because you have challenges does not mean you cannot
overcome them.
Just because you feel neglected does not mean you are not a star.
It just means that you have work to do because what you feel
right now,
Is not the truth about you.

Insights & Reflections

I WILL BE READY

I used to say that I would know him, and he would know me.
I longed for the day that I would be in a loving relationship with
    someone
who truly cared for me.
But something changed within me,
And now I say that I hope I'm ready when he comes.

I've gone through so much—I am exhausted.
I'm tired from trying to make a relationship work that just wasn't
    meant to be.
A relationship that was too hard to make last,
It was slowly killing a part of me.
Now I say—I hope I'm ready when he comes.

I have had great relationships full of joy, excitement, and laughter.
Wonderful experiences that will stay with me forever,
Yet over time I have also experienced tremendous hurt and pain
From a broken heart and empty promises along the way.
So I hope I'm ready when he comes.

I slowly constructed a wall to protect my heart
Vowing not to let another in.
I'm emotionally safe and I like it here.
The pain from previous relationships was too devastating
    tinkering away at my soul

Making it hard for the next man that walked into my life.
I just hope I'm ready when he comes.

I am beginning to slowly heal,
And feeling myself coming alive again.
I'm becoming stronger and able to consider the possibilities.
It's a slow process
So I hope I'm ready when he comes.

If he sees me or talks to me in passing,
And over time he realizes that I just might be the one.
I pray he doesn't give up on me.
That he recognizes just how invaluable and precious I am
And resolves to be patient.

I want him to take my hand and pull me out of my safe space.
I want him to encourage me to take a chance and be receptive to
    love again.
For if he welcomes me with open arms,
And reaffirms that I am the one for him,
Then if I'm not ready when he comes,
I will get ready if he stays.

Insights & Reflections

SISTER-FRIEND

Thank you
For being my angel.
Thank you
For being a true sister-friend.
You understand
That I'm not perfect.
You understand
That I make mistakes.
So thank you
For not judging me.
And thank you for seeing the best in me.
You're phenomenal, you're fabulous.
You're patient and you're kind.
So thank you
For your unconditional love.
Your unwavering support and encouragement
Motivates me to continue to forge ahead
And not give up.
So thank you
For being my angel.
Thank you
For being a true sister-friend.

Insights & Reflections

THIS TIME IS DIFFERENT

You hurt me.
Time and time again,
I allowed you to disregard my feelings,
Trample upon them and disrespect me,
In the most hateful and vile way.
You kicked my self-esteem.
You poked at my confidence,
And discounted my love for you.
But you are not the one to blame,
I am.
I allowed it to happen.
Somewhere, somehow, along the way,
I lost respect for me.
And began to feel like I needed you,
More than you valued me.
And that having something was better than nothing.
How wrong could one person be?
For I did not see you for who you really were,
And I could not see me for what I was destined to be.
You hurt me.
But this time is different.
Because this time I am taking care of me.

Insights & Reflections

THE POWER OF LOVE

What allows us to change the world is love.
It bridges the gap between those who are held in high esteem,
And those that have been cast aside.
It brings comfort to those who have been disappointed by others,
And those who caused the disenchantment.
It conveys support to those who are struggling to survive,
And those that that are in need of encouragement.
It creates a bond between family and friends,
And builds a connection with a complete stranger.
It enables us to appreciate each obstacle and challenge,
While pushing us to grow from the opportunity.
It grants us liberation from the emotional baggage we carry,
And strengthens us to prevail and overcome adversity.
It forces us to reflect on the things we need to change,
Permitting us to be our true authentic self.
It is the power of love.

Insights & Reflections

THRILL OF EXCITEMENT

The thrill of excitement,
From just being alive and waking up to a new day.
It is exhilarating even liberating,
Because I have been fortunate and blessed,
To live and see another day.
Adorned with God's grace and mercy.
What an awesome feeling of gratitude!
What a significant and wondrous gift!

Insights & Reflections

DO YOU SEE ME?

I know you see the color of my skin,
But do you see me?
What lies beneath my exterior?
Do you understand that while my color is a critical part of who
    I am,
It does not begin to define or describe the *whole* me,
The entirety of my soul, spirit, and being,
The essence of who I am and what I have to offer the world.
Do you see me?
I am framed by the experiences that I have had over the years.
Not just as a woman but as a 'woman of color',
Sculpted by my background—my upbringing,
Supplemented by my education.
It provides a context and a lens that has shaped how I view
    the world,
And who I am as a person.
But it alone does not determine how I approach the world.
It does not serve as a guide for how I treat and interact with others.
Instead it forces me to question my biases.
Those judgments and assumptions that I make about others,
Sometimes unconsciously and sometimes consciously.
Having this awareness is instrumental to my growth.
Because it helps me to move past preconceived notions,
Recognizing that if I want others to see me along with the color
    of my skin,

To value the gifts and the talents that I bring,
I must be willing to do the same and embrace the value that
others offer.
Recognizing that none of us are perfect; we all have flaws,
But we also have unbelievable gifts and talents to share with
each other.
Let's seize this opportunity and begin the conversation.
Do you see me?

Insights & Reflections

ALREADY YOURS

What you are destined to have is already yours.
All you have to do is believe that you deserve it,
And do the work necessary to achieve it.
First you have to envision it; see yourself attaining it.
It may not come easy,
But you have what it takes to persevere; so refuse to give up.
If it is indeed your passion,
Don't allow obstacles to scare you away.
And you can't permit the hills and the valleys to cause you to
    sink into despair.
Even though the wall may seem indestructible—you can prevail.
Don't allow your perception to cause you to stand still,
Held captive by fear—which really is just a false representation
    of the outcome.
You can conquer any challenges you encounter.
You may stumble and you may falter,
But all you have to do is get back up again.
Keep moving and repudiate anything or anyone that stands in
    your way,
Because what you are destined to have is already yours.

Insights & Reflections

KINDNESS MAKES A DIFFERENCE

Kindness
Such a simple word but it means so much.
For when you are kind—you take time to support others.
When you are kind—you take the time to encourage others.
When you are kind—you just don't think about yourself.
You extend yourself to others even when you don't feel like it.
Even when you are grappling with uncertain circumstances,
Or feeling the weight of despair.
When you are kind to others,
You will make a difference.
You will significantly impact the people you meet,
And touch the lives of people that you don't directly encounter.
Because your kindness extends forward and multiplies,
Kindness makes a difference.

Insights & Reflections

LOVE UNCONDITIONALLY

How do you love unconditionally,
Especially when you have been hurt so deeply?
How do you move beyond the pain,
When you have been victimized by those closest to you?
How do you recognize the opportunity,
That has been cleverly disguised inside the obstacle?
How can you forgive yourself when you have been angry for
    so long?
How can you forgive others when they have consistently
    disappointed you?
How can you let go of the bitterness and start the healing process?
Recognizing that holding onto grudges does not serve you in a
    positive way.
We all have shortcomings, weaknesses, and imperfections,
But you will be happiest and the most fulfilled,
When you love unconditionally.

Insights & Reflections

BY YOUR ACTIONS

Some people think that love is saying the words 'I love you',
But it's more than that—it's deeper.
Love is a behavior; the way one acts—the way you treat another
person.
The thoughtfulness, respect, kindness, and consideration that
you show,
Yes, even when someone has mistreated you and tried to make
you feel less than.
Especially when your day has gone from bad to worse.
It is your unwillingness to take it out on others.
Love is your acceptance that no one is perfect.
Love is encouraging those around you in the face of obstacles.
It is forgiveness.
It is everything good and everything pure.
And it is the commandment that stands above all others.
Love by your actions.

Insights & Reflections

THE MAN THAT YOU ARE

I always knew there were great men out there,
I just could never seem to meet any of them,
That is until I met you.
The night we met; we had a wonderful conversation
It was full of laughter and jokes yet there were moments of
    intense exchanges.
Your eyes were kind, your smile was gentle, and you
    demonstrated
That you were genuinely interested in getting to know me as
    a person.
How wonderful it feels to be acknowledged,
Appreciated for the person that you are.
And not as a figment of someone's imagination,
Or what they want you to be.
Thank you for seeing me.
Thank you for being the great man that you are.

Insights & Reflections

THINK BIG

Don't allow your thinking to limit you.
Don't let your thinking hold you captive to just 'good enough'
    thoughts.
There is a whole world out there,
Just waiting for you to come forward,
With confidence, dedication, and commitment.
Just waiting for you to recognize who you really are,
And how powerful you can be.
So many wonderful and amazing opportunities await you,
So don't think small—think big!
You were created to make a difference.
You were given the awesome responsibility of sharing your gifts.
Your contributions will be invaluable.
But if you are going to walk in the role created just for you
You have to receive it.
You first have to see it in your mind.
In the core of your soul—you have to know that it is possible.
Believe that you have everything you need because you do.
Don't allow your thinking to limit you.
Think big!

Insights & Reflections

USING WHAT I HAVE

There is so much I want to give,
Yet it is so hard to figure out what others need.
There is so much that I want to say,
Yet my voice fails me and sometimes I'm afraid to speak.
There is so much that I want to do,
Still I am challenged in taking the first step.
But when I take the time to sit and reflect,
I realize that it's not about figuring out the answers to these things.
Instead, the value is in using the talents I have been given.
Believing that my gifts will reach those destined to receive them,
And that they will be touched, guided, encouraged, and supported,
At exactly the time they need it.
So by stepping out and taking a risk,
I am not only helping myself, but I am enabling others to act,
By using what I have.

Insights & Reflections

WHERE IS YOUR BACKYARD?

Where do you go when you need to get away?
Where is your refuge?
Where do you get your strength?
Where is your backyard?
Where do you go when you need peace and solitude?
When you need some balance and harmony—somewhere that
    calms you?
You should always have a safe space reserved just for you,
Where you can just be.
Where is your backyard?
Where do you go when you just need to get away,
To take a break—to be one with nature and with God?
My backyard is that safe haven where I can go.
A retreat to get away from all the chaos of the day.
It is where I get the courage to move forward with fortitude
    and resilience.
It is where I can express my gratitude and appreciation.
It is where I can see endless possibilities.
Where is your backyard?

Insights & Reflections

WORTH THE EFFORT

Sometimes you get stuck in a place and it's difficult to move
forward.
You just need a push—maybe even a gentle shove.
It can be in the form of a friend or family member giving advice
and encouragement,
Or even a stranger sharing some lessons learned.
It can also be something that happens to you or around you.
Whatever it is—it reaffirms that you are on the right path,
And it reminds you that you are not alone and that you can't stop.
Even in your seemingly wilderness experience,
You can make it.
There are actions you can take—tasks you can complete.
Maybe it's a book, an invention, some creative work of art,
Whatever it is—it has your name written on it.
It is designed just for you—and you are the only one that can
move it forward.
It is a task that only you can complete.
So yes sometimes you may get stuck—and yes you may need
a push,
But don't let it be in vain—use it to your advantage.
Dig deeper, climb a little higher, swim a little farther.
Don't give up—your perseverance will produce rich dividends.
You are worth the effort.

Insights & Reflections

YOU HELPED ME TODAY

You helped me without saying a word.
Your life is a witness to God's love and kindness.
I saw you the other day as you were walking,
I watched your expression; you appeared deep in thought.
It was a look of desperation, a look of utter defeat.
Fear was dancing in your eyes.
It was as if you were pondering what to do next.
My heart went out to you.
Because it was something that I was not accustomed to seeing—
    not from you.
But then I saw something truly uplifting—inspiring—motivating,
I saw you look up and mumble something.
I assume you were talking to God
Because as you were looking up; you began to cry.
I heard you whisper the words "It's not going to prosper."
Your expression slowly changed to one of peaceful reassurance.
As if to declare "God, I know you have it."
I was excited just by seeing this small seemingly intimate
    interaction,
Between you and God.
It was a wonderful experience that I needed to witness,
Because it encouraged my heart and motivated me.
You helped me today.

Insights & Reflections

CHART NEW TERRITORY

As you embark on a new and exciting journey,
There are limitless possibilities before you.
You have been granted a unique opportunity to chart new
    territory,
To make a difference and impact all those who come into
    your presence.
What an awesome gift!
To grow, learn, and achieve something even greater,
And even more profound than you could have ever imagined.
Your steps are ordered.
You have always been exactly where you needed to be,
To position you for this amazing and remarkable voyage.
In an environment that needs to hear your voice,
And a setting that craves and longs for fresh and innovative ideas.
They have been awaiting your arrival!
This is your chance to make big bold courageous steps.
Make a choice to embrace each obstacle like the warrior you are.
A stepping stone leading to mountains of success,
Allowing you to chart new territory.

Insights & Reflections

AMAZING SUCCESS

It's a very difficult time for you.
While I can't know exactly how you are feeling,
I do understand how frustrating it can be.
I just hope that you will take a minute
To breathe and take in the true beauty of today
And recognize that you have a choice.
You have an opportunity to learn something new
About yourself, about others, about life.
You can seize this moment for what it was meant to be.
Move forward and refuse to be discouraged,
Forge ahead and dare to be defeated,
Because the best is yet to come.
You have everything you need inside of you.
I know that regardless of where you sit,
Whether it is here or someplace else,
You will always excel—-you will always grow,
And you will always enjoy amazing success.

Insights & Reflections

SHOWING UP

How are you showing up to others?
Do they see a bright light beaming out from within,
Or do they see darkness—a victim surrounded by clouds?
Do they see an expert who always has the answer,
Or do they see a compassionate listener,
Who asks reflective and thought-provoking questions?
Do they see a person who is always focused on self,
Or do they see someone who seeks to bring out the best in those
    around them?
How are you showing up to others?
Do they see someone who values and seeks their input,
Or do they see a person who is closed to suggestions from others?
Do they see someone who is self-aware,
And willing to acknowledge their shortcomings?
Or do they see a person who refuses to accept responsibility?
Do they see someone who is authentic,
Or do they see a false representation of the person standing
    before them?
It's important that we take the time to consider what others see
    when they look at us.
To be attuned to the consequences of both our verbal and non-
    verbal interactions,
To appreciate the talents that each of us brings to an encounter.
It's an awesome opportunity to influence all who come into
    your presence.
How are you showing up to others?

Insights & Reflections

GROW THROUGH YOUR WILDERNESS

We all go through periods of wilderness in our lives,
But it's up to us how we experience each episodic event.
Each one may be different, some more painful than others,
Still, we have a choice and we have options in how we respond.
We can face it timidly with alarming horror and disappointment
    and consequently become depressed.
Or we can make another choice.
We can confront it bravely with unwavering faith, fierce
    determination, and courage,
With the overarching purpose and desire to learn and grow,
    from each wilderness experience.
We can seek the positive in every situation,
Recognizing that each wilderness experience is a development
    opportunity,
Preparing us for something even better than we could ever
    imagine.
So yes, we all go through wilderness experiences,
While it may be challenging for you now—be encouraged,
Use this time to grow through your wilderness.

Insights & Reflections

MY DESTINY

Contemplating my next steps,
Wondering what path I should follow,
Stepping out into a sea of risks, climbing a mountain filled with
    laughter and pain, adorned with heartache and happiness,
Crawling through a tunnel filled with darkness,
Yet the glimpse of a bright light illuminates my soul.
There is a calm, peaceful, and serene feeling of joy and anticipation,
A rainbow of hope, faith, and enduring love,
Floating around me—embedded inside me—speaking to me,
Letting me know that it's not for my purpose for which I do
    these things.
It's a higher purpose—more than I could ever hope or fathom.
It's not what I have planned for my life—it's what my creator has
    planned for me.
It's the presence of something bigger than myself—omnipresent.
Something greater than I will ever be—guiding me.
Pushing me, and assuring me that I am an overcomer.
I am more than a conqueror and I came into the world for such
    a time as this.
As I fulfill my unique purpose,
I fulfill my life's destiny.
And beyond the enormous sea, at the top of the amazing
    mountain,
At the end of the treacherous tunnel,

There is something amazing, dynamic, captivating and glorious
    waiting for me,
That belongs not only to me but to my creator.
Still only I can achieve it because it's my calling.
It is my destiny.

Insights & Reflections

EVEN STRONGER

Challenges in my life have always made me stronger.
Yet when I'm in the moment—experiencing what is,
Sometimes I feel like I'm floundering—slipping—falling.
I'm not at my best.
Sometimes I don't feel like I'm where I need to be.
It's uncomfortable—this place.
It's scary and yet it's a growth opportunity,
Because I don't have to allow it to provide additional stress in
    my life.
I can use it to my advantage.
I can be okay with some discomfort.
In other words, I can make another choice.
I can choose to grow while in the moment.
I can choose to learn along my journey.
I can trust God.
Recognizing that this process will allow me to come out of
    this experience,
Even stronger.

Insights & Reflections

GREAT EXPECTATION

Reluctantly I sit,
Waiting for the unexpected,
Yet hoping that it will not come.
For if it appears,
How will I respond to the challenge,
That it will present?
How will I approach my need for resolution?
And simultaneously,
How will I embrace the opportunity it will offer?
For as I sit and reflect on the moment,
I slowly realize,
That maybe reluctance is not the response,
Instead, perhaps the answer is great expectation.

Insights & Reflections

IF YOU KNEW

If you knew the truth about you,
You would know that you are destined for success.
You would recognize the obstacles you encounter as opportunities.
You would embrace the lessons from every situation.
You would taste the fruit from your harvest.
If you knew the truth about you,
You would know that it is all in your perspective.
You would understand that you have everything that you need
    inside of you.
You would embrace and maximize every moment.
If you knew the truth about you,
You would see yourself as the diamond you are.
You would understand that living life is not about the destination,
Instead, it's about reaping the benefits along the journey.
For if you really knew the truth about you,
You would know that you are destined for success.

Insights & Reflections

IT'S TIME

Deep down,
In the trenches of my soul,
My voice cries out,
Struggling to break through the disarray in my life.
Where am I going?
What path am I destined to travel?
What is my purpose in life?
Where is my happiness?
Where is my joy?
I cry out louder,
Because I know I can.
I have the ability to soar.
I feel my strength fighting to come to the surface,
Encouraging me—take a chance,
Encouraging me—take a risk,
Because I am worth it.
I am unique, I am special,
And yes, I am worth it.
My voice cries out and I know it's time.
It's time for me to stand up.
It's time for me to move forward.
It's time for me to take care of me.

Insights & Reflections

ENJOYING EACH MOMENT

Moments of laughter
Shared between two people
Commemorating the time spent together
Celebrating yet full of caution
Humorous yet full of truth
Sharing yet still protecting inner thoughts and secrets
That can only come in time
When we are secure
When we trust and let go of vulnerabilities
Accepting the imperfections
In order to make each other strong
We are simply enjoying the moment

Insights & Reflections

ONE THAT LOVES ME MOST

Lord you are awesome!
You are all that I need to survive.
Sometimes I waiver, sometimes I stumble,
Still I inherently know,
That I can rise again.
You will never fail me.
You will stand by my side,
Through my doubts and disappointments,
And through my joy and happiness.
What can I say,
About the adoration I have for you?
What can I do,
To express my gratitude for your loving kindness?
For you have done wondrous and amazing things for me!
I'm so grateful, speechless, even to the point
Of tears because when I sit down,
And reflect on your goodness and your mercy,
I am at a loss for words crying tears of joy in my heart.
I feel myself growing closer and closer,
To the one that loves me most!

Insights & Reflections

THORN IN MY SIDE

I have a thorn in my side.
I constantly question myself and my capabilities.
I know that I am smart, and intelligent, and strong,
But sometimes I have a hard time appreciating me for who I am,
And what I have to offer.
Sometimes I have feelings of inadequacy.
That I might not be good enough,
Or pretty enough,
Or smart and intelligent enough,
But God loves me so much!
For in his infinite wisdom and kindness,
He sends others to me to affirm,
Just how special I am,
Just how beautiful, smart and intelligent I am.
Then I realize that I am truly blessed,
I am loved,
Even with this thorn in my side.

Insights & Reflections

PREPARATION TIME

The time of waiting—of preparation,
Can be the most painful, the most stressful, and the most
    emotional.
For as time passes and what you are hoping for does not
    materialize,
You begin to question yourself and you wonder if you did
    the right thing.
Doubt whispers you moved too fast—it cautions you will not
    be successful.
Embarrassment murmurs that you should have stayed in your
    safe space.
Worry nudges you to go back to where you were,
The place where you felt comfortable, secure, and stable,
The place where you had control.
Yet it's the same place where you were not growing.
To be where you are now is scary—even terrifying,
Still internally you just know,
That you are exactly where you need to be.
Because in this place you are finding out just what you are made of,
The insecurities, lack of confidence, and fear,
Are all coming to the surface.
Yet you fight with courageous vigor,
Because you realize that sometimes the most illuminating growth,
Comes from the uncertainty,
The time of waiting—preparation time.

Insights & Reflections

AS I EXPERIENCE

As I experience each day,
I have come to appreciate the life that I have.
I believe that I am where I am supposed to be.
What a gratifying moment!
Yes I have heartaches,
And I have experienced so many disappointments.
But I also have uplifting moments,
Filled with laughter and happiness.
It is simply amazing
To experience God's infinite kindness.
It is something I cannot comprehend.
Yet I willingly accept it.
I embrace it,
As I experience each day.

Insights & Reflections

WHEN YOU ARE EXCITED

When you are excited, it oozes out for all to see.
Your positive energy transforms all in your presence.
They want to be around you—sharing in your space,
Of joy, happiness, and tranquility.
You can handle anything life throws your way,
Because realize that it is not about the challenges you face,
It's your attitude as you weather the storm.
It's about the opportunity to learn something new.
It's about the chance to grow.
To be better, to reach for higher, and to achieve more,
When you are excited,
It oozes for all to see.

Insights & Reflections

NOT WITHOUT A PRICE

Thinking about my life,
The successes and blessings that I continue to experience,
Have not come without a price.
For whom much is given, much is required,
And I'm not exempt—the same rule applies to me.
I am instructed to share my knowledge.
I am required to share my wisdom.
And I am commanded to love and help others,
Yes, even when I don't feel like it.
Especially when I don't want to.
Even when my energy is diminishing day by day,
And the receiver has not been as grateful,
Or as thankful as I think they should be.
I have to remember that to whom much is given, much is required.
For it is really not about me,
It is about serving others.
So while the successes that I experience on a daily basis,
Have not come without a price,
Joy and adoration come from knowing,
That I have been blessed abundantly to have resources.
I will continue to give.
Even if gratitude and appreciation never come,
I must keep reminding myself—that I'm giving what is required,
And it's well worth the price!

Insights & Reflections

I AM STILL HERE

Reflecting on my life
All of the obstacles I have overcome,
Can sometimes be overwhelming.
I am so amazed,
And I'm so taken aback,
When I look around and I see,
Where I am—how far I've come.
It all came together when I realized,
That in all of my experiences, it was not about me.
So I relish in the moment,
Of how extremely blessed one person can be.
Overcome with tears of gratitude,
Joy and thanksgiving,
I have experienced things that others might not understand,
Things that others might not ever experience,
And I am still here.

Insights & Reflections

STANDING STILL

Standing still can be a good thing.
It can be instrumental to growth and development,
Allowing the needed time to refocus and reassess the important
    things in life.
A season of self-reflection,
Where you build awareness of what is not only happening in
    the external world,
But you are also more attuned to inner feelings, thoughts,
    and emotions,
Developing intuitive insights you did not think were possible.
It can also be a time where you begin to question the meaning
    of life.
Your purpose, your destiny, and the gifts that only you can offer,
And whether the path you are walking is indeed yours to walk.
Standing still can be a good thing.
It can be a time of self-awakening.
A time for building up and a time for extending outward.
But the inner growth is the most amazing—it is the most
    rewarding!
It gives you the tools you need to confront adversity.
Along with the tribulations and trials you encounter along the way.
So recognize it for it is—an opportunity.
It can be awesome and character building—especially when
    you realize,
That standing still can be a good thing.

Insights & Reflections

YOU DESERVE IT

What would you do if you had the chance,
To do anything and be the person you dreamed you could be?
What would you do if you had the opportunity,
To realize your goals and your purpose in life?
Would you make a plan to guide you and help orchestrate
    your journey,
Or would you wait for someone to give you direction?
Would you be excited and full of passion,
Or would you be distressed and confused?
Would you take action and move deliberately with purpose,
Or would you sit around and do nothing?
This is your chance.
You can do anything and be anything.
But you have to take action now.
Believe in yourself—be confident in your ability.
You deserve it.

Insights & Reflections

IT TAKES COURAGE

It takes courage to walk through a door when you don't know
what's on the other side.
To expect the best even when you have experienced immense
challenges,
To be confident in your abilities even when others doubt you,
To know that you have everything inside you to be successful.
It takes courage to walk through the door especially when you
are afraid of the outcome.
To step out and take a risk even when you feel compelled to stay
in your safe space,
To challenge yourself even though you feel stretched too thin,
To know that you are destined for greater than where you are,
It takes courage to walk through a door when it has been so hard
to get it to budge.
When you're exhausted by your effort that seems to have
produced no success,
To anticipate what's ahead even though you feel like you are
struggling to stay above the surface,
To reach deep within and see the vision for your future,
It takes courage to walk through a door—but if you do—you just
may find your destiny!

Insights & Reflections

I AM POSITIONED

Reflecting,
Thinking about where I am at this very moment in time.
Trusting God that I am positioned,
Exactly where I need to be.
Even though it's not comfortable,
And honestly, I can't articulate this feeling.
A little scared—a little tense,
I can't find the words to describe it.
Yet in the core of my soul and the innermost parts of my heart,
That place where faith and hope reside,
I feel an overwhelming conviction and I am assured,
That I have grace—I have favor—and I have support.
I know that I am destined for greater,
I just have to remain faithful.
Trusting God I am positioned,
Exactly where I am supposed to be.

Insights & Reflections

FLICKER OF LIGHT

Admiring the sunset from a beautiful day,
Mesmerized by the possibilities of what lies ahead,
Reflecting on the events of the past,
Yet remaining focused on the bright light beaming in front
    of me.
For just above the clouds,
I see the flickering of something more powerful than I could
    ever imagine,
Of something more glorious than I could possibly explain.
And I'm striving to catch a glimpse of what's to be,
Without being caught up in what has been.
I'm forging ahead in spite of my insecurities.
I'm challenging myself—in spite of my fears.
I'm soaring to amazing heights,
Yet I know there's something even greater beyond the light.
For I see the flickering of something more powerful than I could
    ever imagine.
Of something more glorious than I could possibly explain.
I see it—in the flicker of the light.

Insights & Reflections

I HAVE TO LOVE ME TOO

I thought he was the one was for me.
My soul mate—my best friend—my confidante,
That is until I saw the real person.
His flaws and weaknesses were based on his pain,
And nobody's perfect...therefore I thought the relationship
Could and should be salvaged.
Surely we could survive the turmoil,
Of the unkind words and the hurt feelings.
I tried to be patient,
However, I encountered something even more powerful
And detrimental to our relationship.
It was denial and refusal to take responsibility for his actions.
How agonizing was the realization that came from knowing,
That even though we were two smart intelligent individuals,
And yes I believe that we truly loved each other,
Maybe it was not enough.
Our mode of thinking was polar opposite.
We saw the world through different lenses.
He said he was the head, but I couldn't follow where he wanted
    to lead.
And how can two walk together unless they agree.
What a traumatic and heartbreaking experience.
But it would have been even more devastating,
To stay in something that was not emotionally healthy.

To stay in something that didn't lift me up,
And make me feel special.
Something that stopped me from being me.
So I made the decision to leave him,
My final words were "I love you I really do—but when it is all said
     and done,
I have to love me too."

Insights & Reflections

FINALLY

I'm finally realizing that I hold the key to my success.
That I can speak life or death into my life.
That the power of my tongue makes a difference.
My thoughts and actions frame my outcomes.
I'm finally realizing that how I approach obstacles depends
    largely on my attitude.
I determine if I am going to be positive or if I will be negative.
Whether I see obstacles as opportunities or as setbacks.
Whether I see change as something amazing or as the pain I
    have to survive.
My thoughts and actions frame my outcomes.
They make me who I am.
I'm finally realizing that I am destined for something greater.
I have a purpose to fulfill.
I make mistakes and learn lessons along the way.
I embrace the possibilities and look forward to the future.
My thoughts and actions frame my outcomes.
I take life one day at a time.
I'm learning that I hold the key to my success,
Finally.

Insights & Reflections

COME BACK STRONGER

I never thought I would experience,
Such a dreadful time in my life.
Everything I thought was—is no more.
Everything that I have believed in,
Has somehow been taken from me.
I'm disillusioned, disenchanted,
And grappling—struggling to survive.
My friends may have gone through something similar,
But how they possibly understand what I am feeling.
My family loves me unconditionally,
But they can't be there for me right now.
Somehow I have got to overcome this,
And I really don't know how,
Those around me reaffirm my strength,
But I am barely hanging on.
The pain is excruciating.
I am grappling fiercely to hold on,
To the little self-confidence that I have left.
I'm not sure where this path will take me,
But I am going to take it one day at a time,
And trust that I will be okay,
I will get through this,
I will survive and come back stronger.

Insights & Reflections

GOD'S KINDNESS

God's kindness
Is amazing.
It gets me through each day.
His wisdom
Is outstanding
It guides me in making decisions.
His mercy
Is comforting
It makes me believe that I can endure anything.
His grace
Is reassuring
I am forgiven when I make mistakes.
Above all his love
Is unconditional
I feel it every day.

Insights & Reflections

THE GIFT OF YOU

Don't deprive the world of the gift of you!
You have something unique to offer.
Something that only you can share.
It's something that you love.
Something that you feel passionate about.
It's special, it's genuine, and only you can give it.
Don't think that the world is saturated because others have
    similar gifts.
Not so, your gift will make room for you.
It will be received with enthusiasm by those that only you
    can touch.
Don't deprive the world of the gift of you!
There is someone that only you can motivate.
Someone that only you can inspire.
Someone that only you can awaken.
Don't deprive the world of the gift of you!
Keep moving forward in spite of the barriers.
Be patient and use those obstacles as opportunities.
You are an overcomer.
You were destined for this moment.
So don't deprive the world of the gift of you!

Insights & Reflections

INCREDIBLY YOU

I'm sitting here thinking of you,
And how incredible you are.
That you would love me.
That you would think of me.
That you would care enough to send others to me,
To reaffirm just how important,
And just how special I am.
It baffles me that you care so much,
But I'm so thankful.
I'm beyond grateful,
I'm in awe and complete adoration.
So thank you,
For just being incredibly you.

Insights & Reflections

HIGHER PURPOSE

Searching tirelessly for something with an unquenchable thirst.
Seeking to understand the yearning for more than what the eyes
    can see.
Struggling with fear that comes from disappointment,
And insecurities derived from failure after failure.
Yet exploring the possibilities of what lies ahead even when the
    outcome is unknown.
Resting in the uncertainty and discomfort of not having all the
    answers,
Yet still enjoying the solitude of stillness in the midst of noise
    and distractions.
Learning and growing from the opportunity cleverly disguised
    in each obstacle.
Recognizing that I have been called to a higher purpose.

Insights & Reflections

SEE YOURSELF

If you could see yourself the way others see you,
You would understand why people smile when you come into
    their presence.
How they are filled with excitement just by being in the same
    room with you,
How they light up when you talk with them.
They ask about you when you're not there.
You lift them up, encourage them, and make them feel like
    they are special.
They feel your genuine interest and how much you care.
Your authenticity shines through.
Your confidence in them is a source of motivation.
You make a difference in their lives.
And you demonstrate it daily by your actions.
You are simply amazing.
See yourself the way others see you.

Insights & Reflections

IN THE STILLNESS

In the stillness,
That's when God speaks to me.
The time when I get away from the noise and distractions,
Allowing his soft voice to whisper in my ear.
That's when he provides me the directions that I need to follow.
In the stillness,
That is when I take the time to listen and seek his presence.
He comforts me and gives me peace in the midst of the turbulence.
And even though I don't have control over the circumstances,
I feel a sense of calm because I trust him.
My approach changes, I adjust my attitude.
He gives me the strength I need to persevere.
To move forward in spite of the chaos.
In the stillness,
My creator talks to me—he offers me guidance.
To come out of the haze,
Leading me to a place of clarity—I call it refuge.
In the stillness,
I see things that I may not have seen before.
New perspectives appear in the silence.
In the stillness,
I embrace changes and transitions with courage.
I give myself permission to just 'be' and 'wait'.
His voice is a beacon of light,
In the stillness.

Insights & Reflections

CPSIA information can be obtained
at www.ICGtesting.com
Printed in the USA
LVHW092225280521
688849LV00001B/8